BE A SCIENTIST
INVESTIGATING
LIGHT

JACQUI BAILEY

WAYLAND
www.waylandbooks.co.uk

First published in Great Britain in 2019 by Wayland
Copyright © Hodder & Stoughton, 2019
The text in this book was previously published
in the series 'Investigating Science'

Credits
Series Editor: Julia Bird
Illustrator: Ed Myer
Packaged by: Collaborate

HB ISBN 978 1 5263 1133 7
PB ISBN 978 1 5263 1134 4

Wayland
An imprint of
Hachette Children's Group
Part of Hodder & Stoughton
Carmelite House
50 Victoria Embankment
London EC4Y 0DZ

An Hachette UK Company
www.hachette.co.uk

Printed in China

MIX
Paper from
responsible sources
FSC® C104740
FSC
www.fsc.org

BE A SCIENTIST

INVESTIGATING LIGHT

WAYLAND

www.waylandbooks.co.uk

CONTENTS

WHAT IS LIGHT?

Light lets us see things. Without light we would not be able to see anything at all.

THINK about the differences between light and dark.

- In the daytime, it is light outside and things are easy to see.
- It is hard to see at night in the dark. We use electric lights to help us.

How well can you see without light?

YOU WILL NEED
A blindfold
(e.g. a scarf or pillowcase)
A friend
Some small 'mystery' objects
A cake tin or a box with a lid

WHAT CAN YOU SEE IN THE DARK?

1 Sit on the floor. Ask your friend to tie the blindfold over your eyes. Make sure you cannot see anything.

"BECAUSE...

You cannot see what your objects are when you are blindfolded because the blindfold has blocked out the light. Light lets us see. Seeing is one of our five **senses**. When there is no light, we use some of our other senses, such as touch or smell, to find out what things are."

4 Slowly lift the blindfold. How far do you have to lift it before you can see if you were right?

3 Double check that there is no light coming through the blindfold. Open the tin or box and take out the objects, one at a time. Try to find out what they are by feeling them. Tell your friend what you think each mystery object is.

2 Ask your friend to put the 'mystery' objects inside the tin or box and close the lid.

HOW DO WE SEE?

We see when light gets inside our eyes.

THINK about how you see.
- When your eyelids are open, light enters your eyes through the dark hole in the middle, called the **pupil**.
- When your eyelids are closed, no light can enter the pupil and you cannot see.

Does the amount of light make a difference to how well you see?

YOU WILL NEED
A mirror
A pencil and paper
A darkened room
A watch or mobile phone

HOW DOES LIGHT CHANGE YOUR EYES?

1 Look at your eyes in the mirror.

2 Make a drawing of your eyes to show how big the pupils are compared to the rest of your eye.

3 Sit in a room that is quite dark for 3 minutes. Take a watch or mobile phone with you to time yourself.

4 Go back into normal light and immediately look at your pupils again. Compare them with your drawing. Is there a difference? What happens to your pupils as you look in the mirror?

"BECAUSE...

Your pupils are larger after being in the dark because they change size depending on how much light there is around you. When it is dark, they open up as wide as they can to let in as much light as possible. In very bright light, they become as small as they can to stop the bright light damaging the inside of your eyes. "

BRIGHT AS DAY

During the day, the **Sun** gives us all the light we need.

Bright lights can hurt your eyes. The Sun's light is the brightest light of all. Never look directly at the Sun because it could make you blind.

THINK about the light from the Sun.

- On a sunny day, things look bright and clear.
- When it is cloudy, everything looks duller but we can still see.

How strong do you think the Sun's light is?

YOU WILL NEED

A pencil
A sheet of paper

Object water	Sunny sparkly	Cloudy dull

HOW STRONG IS SUNLIGHT?

1 Go outside on a day when it is sunny but there are also clouds in the sky.

2 Look around you. How does everything look when the Sun is shining? Make a list as shown here, and note how clearly you can see things. What do the colours look like? Do some things sparkle?

BECAUSE...

When there are clouds in the sky the daylight is dim and colours are less bright. This is because the clouds are blocking out some of the Sun's light. But clouds cannot block out all of the Sun's light because it is too strong.

The Sun's light is the strongest type of light. It spreads for millions and millions of kilometres throughout space.

3 Wait for the Sun to go behind a cloud. Now look around you again. What differences can you see? Write them down.

4 Look at the picture above. How do you think this picture would change if the Sun went behind a cloud?

11

LIGHT AT NIGHT

At night-time, or in places where sunlight cannot reach, we use **artificial light sources** – things that give us light.

YOU WILL NEED
A pencil and paper
A ruler

THINK about sources of light other than the Sun.
• We use torches to help us see in the dark.
• We use electric lights in our homes.
What other sources of light are there?

HOW MANY LIGHT SOURCES CAN YOU FIND?

1 Divide your piece of paper into three columns.

2 In the first column, make a list of all the things that give out light, both indoors and outdoors. For example: house lights, fires, candles and computer screens.

house light	electricity	1
candle		
firework		

3 In the second column, write down what makes each light source work. For example: electricity, burning. Ask an adult if you are not sure.

4 In the third column, give each light source a mark out of 3 for its level of brightness: 1 = dazzling, 2 = easy to see by, 3 = hard to see by.

12

"BECAUSE...

Some things that shine brightly are not light sources. They do not make their own light, but bounce - or **reflect** - light from elsewhere. The **Moon** reflects light from the Sun, for example. See pages 16-17."

"BECAUSE...

Some lights are brighter than others because they are more powerful. The brightest lights are usually electric lights. Light that comes from a burning candle or wood is weak and may not last very long."

5 Which light sources are the brightest?

TRAVELLING LIGHT

Light travels outwards from its source in straight lines.

YOU WILL NEED

2 pieces of cardboard about 20-30 cm square
A pencil and ruler
A knitting needle
Sticky tack
A torch
A room you can darken

THINK about how you can see lines of light.

• A beam of light from a torch is straight - it does not curve or bend.
• In woodland you can sometimes see lines, or beams, of sunlight shining through the branches of the trees.
Can you see how light travels?

HOW DOES LIGHT TRAVEL?

1 Find the centre of both squares of cardboard by drawing across them from corner to corner, as shown.

CENTRE

2 Use the knitting needle to make matching holes in the centre of both squares. Line the squares up so that you can see through both holes. Prop them in position with sticky tack.

3 Darken the room and shine the torch through both holes. Do you see a beam of light passing between them and through the hole in the last square? Adjust the squares until you do.

4 Now move one of the squares a few centimetres to one side. What happens?

BECAUSE...

When you move one square sideways, the beam of light no longer shines through the last hole. This is because light cannot bend or curve to the side to shine through the hole.

BOUNCING LIGHT

Most of the light we see is reflected, or bounced, off the things around us.

THINK about how different things reflect light.
• A smooth, polished table looks shiny.
• A rough brick wall looks dull.
Which surface reflects the most light?

WHICH SURFACES SHINE THE MOST?

1 Spread your objects on the floor of a darkened room. Shine the torch on them one at a time.

2 Which objects shine the most? Do any of them still shine when the torch is switched off?

" BECAUSE...

Smooth, flat surfaces shine the most because light from the torch bounces off them straight into your eyes. Light bounces off rough surfaces too, but it is scattered by the bumps in the surface so they appear dull. None of the objects shine in the dark, because they do not make any light of their own. "

Reflective surfaces change the direction of light. Try this investigation.

CAN YOU MAKE LIGHT TURN A CORNER?

1 Stand just behind an open door.

2 Hold a hand mirror out in front of you and angle it until you can see what is on the other side of the door.

light

you

light from behind the door bounces off the mirror

"BECAUSE...

You can see what is on the other side of the door because the light from that side hits the mirror and bounces off it at an angle, into your eyes. "

17

BLOCKING LIGHT

Light passes through some things, but not through others.

THINK about what happens when light is blocked.
- Bricks block light so you cannot see through walls.
- Glass does not block light. It is used to make windows and doors.

What other materials block out light?

YOU WILL NEED

Scissors

A shoe box

A ruler

A small toy

A hand torch

Sticky tape

A book

Some test materials (e.g. pieces of paper, cloth, clear plastic, cling film, aluminium foil, tissue paper)

A pencil and paper

WHICH MATERIALS BLOCK OUT LIGHT?

1 Ask an adult to cut a hole about 15 cm x 10 cm in the top of the shoe-box lid, and a square of about 3 cm in one side of the shoe box.

2 Put the toy inside the box and put the lid on.

3 Position the end of the torch over the hole in the side and tape it securely to hold it in place. You may need to rest the torch on something, such as a book. Switch on the torch.

4 Lay your test materials, one at a time, over the hole in the lid, completely covering it. What can you see? Make a record of the results.

" BECAUSE...

You can see the torchlight and toy clearly through some materials. This is because almost all the light passes through these materials, from inside and outside the box. These materials are **transparent**.

Some materials let some light through them and block (reflect) the rest. You can see the torchlight glowing inside the box, but you cannot see the toy very clearly. These materials are **translucent**.

The other materials block all of the light, both from outside and inside the box. You cannot see inside the box at all. These materials are **opaque**.

"

MAKING SHADOWS

When an object blocks out light it makes a **shadow**.

THINK about how objects make shadows.
- Look under your bed. Is it dark there? The darkness is a shadow made by the bed.
- Turn on a desk lamp. Do the objects under the light have shadows? How do objects make shadows?

YOU WILL NEED
The shoe box and book from pages 18–19
A paintbrush and some black paint
A large plastic comb
Sticky tape
A torch

HOW ARE SHADOWS MADE?

1. Remove the lid, toy and torch from the shoe box. Paint the inside of the box black.

" BECAUSE...

You see stripy shadows in the box because the teeth of the comb block the torchlight. Light travels in straight lines - it cannot bend around the teeth to shine behind them.

Some shadows are stronger than others. A glass tumbler is transparent - it will make a shadow but the shadow is weak. Put something solid, such as a straw, inside the glass and you will see its shadow through the glass. A china mug is opaque. It blocks light, so its shadow is strong. If something is inside the mug you cannot see its shadow through the mug. **"**

2 Tape the plastic comb over the hole in the side of the box.

3 Position your torch on the book and shine it through the comb and through the hole. What can you see?

SHADOW SHAPES

An object's shadow is a similar shape to the object.

THINK about how shadows look.

- The shadow a ball makes is round like the ball.
- The shadow your hand makes is shaped like your hand.

Can shadows change their shape?

YOU WILL NEED

A helpful adult

Scissors

The same shoe box as before

A plain white plastic bag

Sticky tape

A book

A small torch

A chair

Some friends

A collection of small objects

WHAT SHAPES DO SHADOWS MAKE?

1 Ask an adult to cut out the base of the shoe box, leaving a 2-cm rim.

2 Cut a piece of plastic bag to cover the base of the box. Stretch the plastic over the base and tape it firmly around the sides. This is your screen.

3 Stand the box upright with the screen facing away from you. Put a book inside it to weigh it down.

4 Place the torch behind the screen so that it shines into the box. It may need to rest on something.

5 Ask your friends to sit in front of the screen. Darken the room. Put each object, one at a time, in front of the torch so that it makes a shadow on the screen.

6 Can your friends guess what each object is? Move the object closer to the torch and then further away. What happens to its shadow?

BECAUSE...

Shadows can play tricks on your eyes because all you see is a flat outline of the object. If the object is turned at an angle to the light, the shadow you see may be squashed or stretched out. If an object is close to the light source, its shadow is larger. If it is further away, its shadow is smaller.

SUN AND SHADOW

Shadows happen outdoors, too.

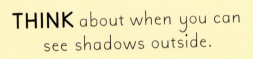

THINK about when you can see shadows outside.

- Are there shadows on a cloudy day?
- Are there shadows on a sunny day? What kinds of shadow does sunlight make?

YOU WILL NEED
A sunny day
A friend

" BECAUSE...
The best shadows happen on clear, sunny days when the Sun's light shines directly on the ground. Any object that stands between the Sun and the ground forms a shadow on the opposite side to the Sun. "

HOW DOES THE SUN MAKE SHADOWS?

1 Go outside with a friend on a sunny day. What shadows do you see?

2 Stand in an open space with your back to the Sun. Where is your shadow?

HOW DO THE SUN'S SHADOWS CHANGE?

1 Stand outside in a sunny spot early in the morning. Ask a friend to make a chalk mark on the ground where your shadow ends.

2 Come back to the same spot at midday and mark your shadow again. Has it changed?

YOU WILL NEED
A friend
An open spot
Chalk

" BECAUSE...

Your shadow is longer in the early morning because the Sun is low down in the sky. At midday, the Sun is almost straight above you and your shadow is much shorter. It is also pointing in a different direction. Why is that? "

25

SHIFTING SHADOWS

Shadows from sunlight point in different directions at different times of day.

THINK about how the Sun's shadows change.
• Which side of your house is in shadow in the morning?
• Which side is in shadow in the evening?
Have the shadows moved?

YOU WILL NEED
A sunny morning
A sheet of card
A straight stick
Sticky tack
An open piece of ground
A ruler and a marking pen
A clock

HOW DO THE SUN'S SHADOWS MOVE?

1 Start early in the morning.

2 Make a hole in the middle of the card. Push the stick through the card and into the ground so it is held in place.

3 Use the ruler and the marking pen to draw along the stick's shadow on the card. Write the time at the end of the shadow. Be careful not to move the card or the stick.

4 Come back every two hours. Mark where the shadow is each time and write the time down. How does the stick's shadow move during the day?

Long ago, people used the movement of the Sun's shadows to tell the time. Shadow clocks are called sundials.

9:00 A.M.

" BECAUSE...

Shadows always point away from the light source that is making them. The stick's shadow moved around the card because the direction of the Sun's light changed during the day. "

27

USEFUL WORDS

Artificial
things are made by people – they do not exist naturally. For example, candles and electric lights would not exist if we did not make them.

Light sources
are things that make light. The Sun is a natural light source. Electric lamps, car lights, candles and firelight are all artificial light sources.

Natural light sources
There are other natural light sources as well as the Sun. A few animals, such as glow-worms and fireflies, make their own light. Lightning is a short but very powerful burst of natural light.

Opaque
materials are things that we cannot see through at all. They reflect all of the light that falls on them. Stone and wood are opaque materials. Most of our clothes are opaque, too!

Pupils
are the dark holes in the middle of the coloured parts of our eyes. Light shines through our pupils onto the back of our eyeballs. Our brain then tells us what we are seeing.

Reflected light
is the light that bounces off the surface of things. We see things because light is bouncing off them and into our eyes. Mirrors reflect light so well that we see a perfect, reversed copy of ourselves when we look into them.

Senses
allow us to find out what is happening around us. We have five senses – they are seeing, hearing, touching, tasting and smelling.

Shadows

are the dark areas that form behind objects when they block out light.

The Sun

is a gigantic ball of glowing gas that gives out great amounts of light and heat. It is more than 100 times bigger than the Earth and is about 150 million kilometres away. It takes eight minutes for light from the Sun to reach Earth.

Translucent

materials allow us to see light through them, but not much else. These materials let some light pass through them but they reflect the rest. Tracing paper and frosted glass are translucent.

Transparent

materials are things that we can see through clearly. Most of the light that falls on them passes through them. Glass and water are transparent.

Sundials

Long ago people used sundials to tell the time. Sundials work using shadows cast by the Sun's light. These shadows change during the day because the Earth is turning. It takes 24 hours for the Earth to make a complete turn.

The Moon

The Moon is a ball of rock that travels around the Earth. We see it in the sky because the Sun's light bounces off it and shines down to Earth. Unlike the Sun, the Moon does not make any light of its own.

MORE INFORMATION

BOOKS

Moving Up with Science: Light by Peter Riley (Franklin Watts, 2016)
Science in a Flash: Light by Georgia Amson-Bradshaw (Wayland, 2018)

WEBSITES

Find out more about light, how it travels and how it gets inside our eyes at:
www.bbc.com/bitesize/topics/zbssgk7

Explore light, translucent and opaque objects and colour at:
https://www.bbc.com/bitesize/topics/znmmn39

PLACES TO VISIT

Take a trip from the dark into light, discovering the many wonders of light and colour along the way at The Observatory Science Centre in East Sussex.

NOTE TO PARENTS AND TEACHERS:

Every effort has been made by the publisher to ensure that these websites contain no inappropriate or offensive material. However, because of the nature of the internet, it is impossible to guarantee that the content of these sites will not be altered. We strongly recommend that internet access is supervised by a responsible adult.

INDEX